Animal Lives

SHARKS

WITHDRAWN

Sally Morgan

QEB Publishing

Published in the United States by
QEB Publishing, Inc.
23062 La Cadena Drive
Laguna Hills
Irvine
CA 92653

Library of Congress Control Number:
2004101323

ISBN 1-59566-034-8

Written by Sally Morgan
Designed by Tall Tree Books
Editor Christine Harvey
Map by PCGraphics (UK) Ltd

Creative Director Louise Morley
Editorial Manager Jean Coppendale

Printed and bound in China

Picture credits

Key: t = top, b = bottom, m = middle,
c = center, l = left, r = right

Ecoscene/Phillip Colla front cover, 4, 5, 11, 14,
18, 22–23, 25, /V&W Brandon Cole 5, 13,
/V&W Kelvin Aitken 6m, 7m, 16t, /Reinhard
Dirsherl 6–7, 9b, 29, /John Lewis 8–9, 15,
/Chinch Gryniewicz 10, /Papilio, Robert Pickett
24, /27t, /Robert Baldwin 28;

Getty Images/Stephen Frink title page, 19,
/Jeff Rotman 12, 20, /Jeff Hunter 16–17,
/Cousteau Society 21, 26–27, /Stone, Chuck
Davis 27t.

The words in **bold** are explained in the Glossary on page 31.

Contents

The shark

Sharks are some of the most amazing creatures in the ocean. Although they are a type of fish, sharks are also vertebrates, which means that they have a backbone. On the top of their backs sharks have a large, triangle-shaped fin that sticks up out of the water when they swim near the surface. They have two large **pectoral fins**, one on each side of their body, behind the **gill slits**. They have other fins, too.

This blue shark has five gill slits on each side of its head.

Sharks have very wide jaws and some types have jagged, pointed teeth.

shark

The biggest-ever great white shark was 23 feet long and weighed about 1,450 pounds. Some sharks have very rough skin, but it protects them, just like a suit of armor.

facts

Sharks use their **gills** to breathe in water. When they breathe, water enters their mouth. The water flows between their gills and out through the gill slits on the sides of their head.

5

Shark types

With more than 360 different **species**, divided into 30 separate families, sharks range incredibly in size, from as small as a person's hand to bigger than a bus. Surprisingly, more than half of all sharks are less than a yard long. The largest sharks, such as the whale shark and the hammerhead shark, are found far out in the open seas and oceans.

The carpet shark uses **camouflage** to blend in with the seabed.

Leopard sharks are slender and covered in brown spots. They grow to more than 6 feet long.

Rare and common sharks

Some types of shark are very rare indeed, such as the megamouth. The dogfish shark and the bull shark are much more common.

shark

The largest shark is the whale shark, which grows up to 50 feet long. The smallest types are the dwarf dogshark and the spined pygmy shark, both of which grow to just 7 inches long.

fact

Tiger sharks are large and can measure up to 20 feet long. They are found in warm seas.

7

Where do you find sharks?

Sharks are found in all the oceans of the world, apart from the coldest waters of the Antarctic. Although some sharks remain in the same region for their entire lives, others swim from ocean to ocean.

Areas where sharks are found.

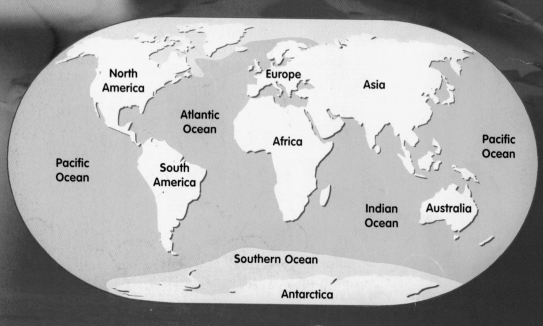

North America

Europe

Asia

Atlantic Ocean

Africa

Pacific Ocean

Pacific Ocean

South America

Indian Ocean

Australia

Southern Ocean

Antarctica

8

Where do sharks live?

Many sharks live their whole lives in the open ocean, thousands of miles from land. Some of the smallest sharks, such as the dogfish, can be found in shallow waters at the beach.

Living in the ocean

Some sharks stay close to the ocean floor, for example wobbegongs and angel sharks. Both types of shark have flattened bodies that are well **camouflaged**, which means they can hide unseen on the seabed. Other sharks live deep in the ocean, hidden in the dark water during the day and feed on the surface at night.

Coral reefs and warm seas are home to the white-tipped reef shark.

9

Beginning life

After mating, a female shark produces only a few large-sized eggs. Most sharks keep their eggs safely inside their body until they are ready to give birth to live young. But some sharks lay their eggs outside their body, and each egg is protected by a tough case. Inside the case, there is a large yolk which supplies food for the baby shark until it is ready to **hatch**.

The dogfish shark's egg attaches itself to rocks or seaweed so that it does not float off into deep water.

shark

Spiny sharks are pregnant for two years. The great white shark gives birth to only one or two pups, but blue and whale sharks can have more than 100 in one go!

facts

Baby sharks

Baby sharks are called pups and look like miniature adult sharks. They even have a full set of teeth. As soon as they are born, they can take care of themselves.

Hammerhead sharks gather in large shoals during the breeding season.

Growing up

As soon as shark pups are born, they swim away from their mother. It is important that they leave the parent very quickly because some female sharks eat their own pups.

Sharks grow slowly and may take many years to become a full-sized adult. They then continue to grow throughout their life.

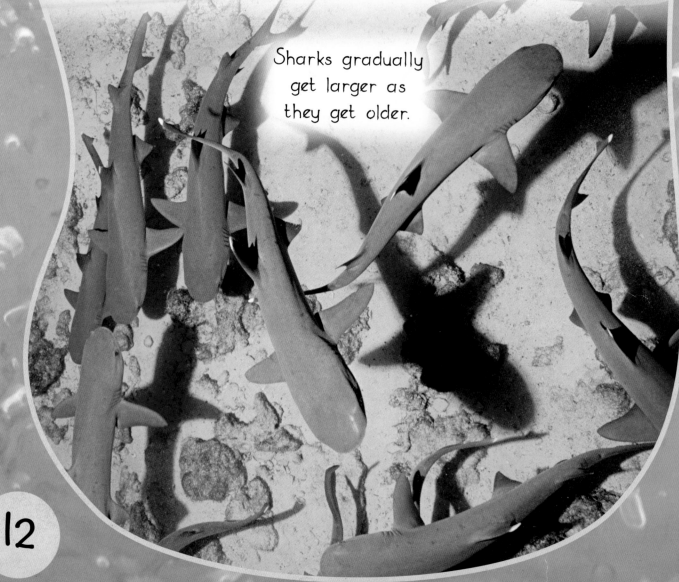

Sharks gradually get larger as they get older.

How long do sharks live?

Nobody is sure how long sharks live. Most of them probably live for less than 25 years, but a few types of shark have been known to live for much longer.

Some of the larger species of female shark are not ready to breed until the female is between 6 and 18 years old. Most females produce eggs every two years.

This great white shark has a lot of scars and may be very old.

Large pectoral fins behind the gill slits help with balance.

Swimming

A shark must keep swimming or it will sink. Some types, such as the great white shark, push themselves through the water using the force of their powerful tails. Other sharks, for example the whale shark, thrust their bodies from side to side to propel themselves through the water. Their large fins help them to balance while swimming.

shark

Some of the fast sharks can cut through the water at speeds of up to 40 mph.

fact

Swimming backward

Sharks cannot swim backward because their large **pectoral fins** are not able to bend upward like other fish. If a shark needs to move backward, it allows itself to be carried back by the water or swims back around in a circle. Sharks must swerve to the side to avoid hitting something, as they cannot stop moving.

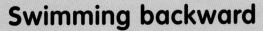

A horn shark resting on the seabed.

This group of Port Jackson sharks are resting in a cave.

Predators

Sharks are **predators**. This means that they hunt and eat other animals in order to survive. Although sharks eat a variety of foods, their diet is mainly made up of fish and **invertebrates**, such as squid and octopus. The larger sharks can catch bigger **prey**, including turtles, seals and even dolphins. Other sharks eat animals that live on the seabed, such as crabs, starfish, sea urchins, and sea anemones.

A horn shark takes a meal of squid eggs on the sea floor.

What do sharks eat?

A hungry shark is not very fussy about its food. In fact it will eat almost anything it finds, including any dead animals that it finds floating in the ocean. Tiger sharks are possibly the least choosy of the **species** and eat the most varied diet. Not only do they catch live animals, such as fish and seals, they will even feed on garbage!

This large shark is surrounded by smaller fish. Fish is a favorite food of most sharks.

shark

An unusual variety of objects has been found in sharks' stomachs, including parts of cows, dogs, penguins, wristwatches, tin cans—even shoes!

fact

Hunting

Sharks hunt in different ways and many attack their **prey** from below. The hungry shark lurks in the deep water where it cannot be seen. Then, when it spots its prey, the shark races after it at great speed, charging upwards out of the darkness of the deep. When hunting, the thresher shark takes full advantage of its long, sturdy tail. Once it spots a shoal of fish, it uses its tail to herd the fish together. Next it stuns them with powerful slaps, again using its mighty tail.

Some sharks lie in wait for their prey.

Hunting groups

Although most sharks hunt alone, a few **species** hunt in packs. Groups of sand tiger sharks, for example, herd shoals of fish into shallow water where they can attack them more easily. Shark pups have to learn to hunt on their own, and many die before they are fully grown.

Shark

After eating a large meal weighing 65 pounds, a great white shark will not need to eat for another 45 days.

fact

Hunting in groups helps sharks catch prey.

Shark teeth

A shark's teeth can be big or small, sharp or blunt, jagged or smooth. The shape of its teeth will have **adapted** to the type of food it eats. Flat teeth are suitable for crunching snails, crabs, and sea urchins, while jagged teeth are ideal for chewing larger animals. A shark's jaws are only loosely connected to its skull, so it can open its mouth extremely wide to swallow large **prey**.

As sharks get older, their teeth get larger. So the oldest sharks have the largest teeth.

Every time a shark catches prey, it loses a few teeth. These are quickly replaced by new ones.

Replacing teeth

Shark pups are born with a full set of teeth already in place. They are the same as adult teeth, but smaller. All sharks have several rows of teeth, but most use only their front row when feeding. The other rows are replacement teeth, to use when the original teeth wear away or falls out. Some types of shark use as many as 30,000 teeth during their lifetime.

Plankton eaters

The whale shark is not only the largest shark in the world, it is also the world's biggest fish. Both the whale shark and the giant basking shark are **filter feeders**, so they eat the tiny plants and animals, called **plankton**, that float in the water.

Whale sharks have enormous **gill slits**, which stretch almost all the way around their heads.

A whale shark is about 15 yards long and makes the diver swimming beside it look tiny.

Eating without teeth

Filter-feeding sharks do not have any teeth. They feed by swimming steadily forward with their huge mouths wide open, scooping up water and **plankton** as they go. The sea water flows through their **gills** where it is filtered. Then the shark eats the food that is trapped.

Shark senses

Sharks use their senses to detect **prey**, especially their senses of smell and sight. Sharks can detect blood in the water from a distance of a mile or two. They can even pick up the sounds and **vibrations** of animals moving in the water hundreds of yards away. As they get closer to their prey, sharks use their eyes to find it

shark

Some sharks may be able to track their prey by smell from up to a mile away, by following a trail of tiny particles of blood.

fact

Sharks like this sand tiger shark make use of all their senses when they are tracking prey.

Sensing movement

The front of a shark's head is called a snout. It is a little like the human nose. The **ampullae of Lorenzini** on the shark's snout are highly sensitive and can detect the electric signals that are produced when other animals move their muscles. This sense means that a shark can detect animals in the water, even if they are hidden.

The hammerhead shark has a very oddly shaped head. Its eyes are about a yard apart.

Sharks and people

Many people are scared of being attacked by sharks when they are in the water, but most sharks are harmless. Only about forty **species** have been known to attack humans. The world's four most dangerous sharks are the great white, tiger, bull, and white-tipped reef sharks.

shark

Each year there are between 70 and 100 shark attacks in the world.

fact

Many people fear great white sharks, however, tiger sharks are more dangerous.

26

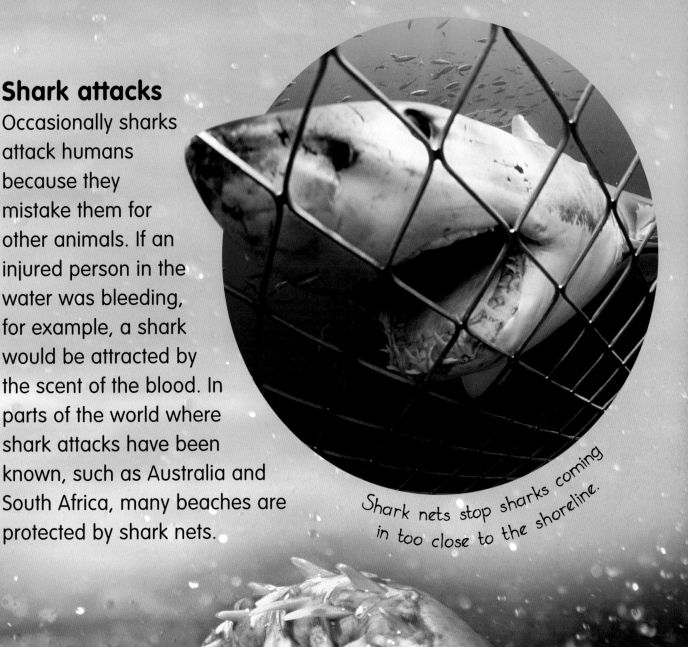

Shark attacks

Occasionally sharks attack humans because they mistake them for other animals. If an injured person in the water was bleeding, for example, a shark would be attracted by the scent of the blood. In parts of the world where shark attacks have been known, such as Australia and South Africa, many beaches are protected by shark nets.

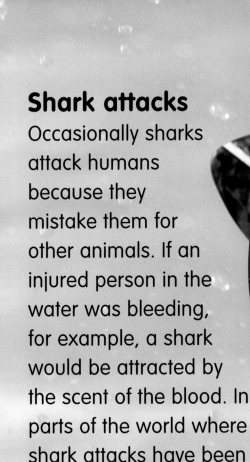

Shark nets stop sharks coming in too close to the shoreline.

27

Sharks under threat

Many sharks are killed for their fins, which are used to make shark fin soup. Large sharks breed slowly and, if they are **overfished,** their numbers quickly fall. The United States and the European Union have banned **shark finning** to protect the shark population.

In some places sharks are threatened because there is too much fishing in general, and not enough food left for the sharks to eat.

Only the fins are needed for shark fin soup, and often the rest of the shark's body is simply tossed back into the sea.

On organized trips, divers can get up close to sharks.

Don't be scared of sharks!

Many people are afraid of sharks, but these amazing animals are an important part of the ocean system. Shark tourism encourages people to get to know sharks better. On some coral reefs, food is left out to attract sharks so divers can get close to them. Shark tourism earns money for local people and means that the sharks are less likely to be killed.

shark
As many as 100 million sharks may be caught every year for their fins.
fact

Life cycle

Female sharks produce eggs. Some sharks lay their eggs in the water, others give birth to live young. The eggs hatch into tiny sharks called pups.

Sharks grow slowly throughout their life.

But many sharks die before they are fully grown. Most sharks do not live more than 25 years.

A shark egg case

Young sharks look like miniature adults and grow slowly.

This old shark has lots of scars.

Glossary

adapted an animal that has adapted has changed to suit the environment in which it lives

ampullae of Lorenzini tiny sensors near the front of a shark's head. These detect electrical signals produced when an animal moves

camouflage an animal's coloring that blends in with its background

filter feeder an animal that sieves, or removes, food such as small plants and animals from the water to eat

gills organs inside the body that are used to take in oxygen from water

gill slits slits, or gaps, in the body wall where water passes out of the body

hatch to break out of an egg

invertebrate an animal without a backbone

overfishing taking too many fish from the ocean

pectoral fins fins that are positioned just behind the gill slits

plankton tiny plants and animals that float in the upper layers of the ocean

predator an animal that hunts other animals

prey an animal that is hunted and eaten by other animals

shark finning the removal of fins from the body of a shark for use in soup

species a group of individuals which have the same appearance and are able to breed and produce young together

vibration a disturbance in the water caused by a moving object or animal

Index